Beware

Shatima Jones

Published by Spines Publishing Platform
ISBN: 979-8-89691-141-8

Beware

Contents

THE PLAYER

We all know about men who have a bunch of women the guy who cant look down. He notices every woman that walks through the room and scopes to find the one who will fall for the lies. Yes, this man is a liar even when he is telling the truth, he is lying. Why? Because he is selfish. So selfish he will not give himself to one person. We all know him as the one who can't stay the night, the one who only answers when its convenient. This dude is something else; he could care less if you leave because there is always another waiting. When y'all are together, he will treat you as if you are the only one when he is just doing whatever to keep you around.

The definition is a confident, successful man with many sexual partners. I love the dictionary, but really. This dude may be confident ok yes, he probably is fine as hell successful hmmmmm maybe. He is all about aggressively chasing woman for his short sexual relationships. He may have money, but is he tricking? He is the hunter, and you are the prey he listens so well, and you thought he was getting to know you. Nah, bookie, he spent money on a bottle to get you drunk, let you talk and waited on that vulnerable opportunity to stick his OPP popsicle in your pudding cup. Guess what though once it's melted, it's gone.

I personally think this guy is insecure, low self-esteem I mean, he is chasing all these women because somewhere in his childhood he was damaged. Men never want to admit they have childhood trauma that damaged them. I bet money this guy has numerous siblings. When you ask him "How many brothers and sisters do you have? his answer will be "I got two sisters on my mom's side and twenty brothers and sisters on my dad's side. I know you are laughing but am I lying? He wants to increase his social status he craves that validation and attention. This guy is just scared of commitment and any kind of intimacy. He claims he doesn't eat pussy, but I bet his ass wants some head. He will never kiss you because that's too much and bending you over will be his forte. Any other way may be too much. The point is he is emotionless. He may like you sex will be good; however, after a few nights he will be gone. You can't ask him for shit because guess what he is not your man he is just the guy you slept with. Hopefully, he will speak next time he sees you and pray he is not with another girl. Don't act up in the end, you will embarrass yourself. Don't do it sis.

The women are a bit different as players. The mindset is different, and in the society we live in, women would be considered "whores" for having more than one man the double standard is crazy. Men are just mad because women do it better but isn't that with everything? See, women don't just date a bunch of men for sex not by a long shot every dude has a purpose. Women make a team let me explain. There is the food guy the one they call when they are hungry, so he probably gets a call during work hours for lunch, maybe a date dinner from time to time. If she doesn't have a car then there is the ride guy yup, he is called just for that to get her where she needs to be when there is no other option of transportation.

Then there is the chill guy, the one she calls when she wants to hang out, maybe go to the bar to have a few drinks and best believe he is paying for it. There is also the guy she never calls he is just there aka the flunky. He calls her trying to be involved you know the one who texts every morning "Grand rising queen" ughhh annoying. She may pick up the phone for him when she is bored, he will always be the last resort.

Last but never least is the booty call. Even though those other guys may seem cool, no one compares to the "booty call." This is the only guy who can get the pearl. He is probably somebody she has known for a long time and for her, whatever he can offer she doesn't want he is good for one thing and one thing only. He only gets late-night calls or leaves the club drunk calls. He enjoys it as much as she does.

In reality, if we called it equal to a man this would be Pimping. The definition of a pimp in the dictionary is a criminal who is associated with, usually exerts control over, and lives off the earnings of one or more prostitutes' Criminal is a bit much I don't they are criminals however the control over the other person is definite. She has her bottom dudes and the other workers on the team. Just as a man would have his bottom bitch vs the other whores on his team. My personal opinion woman do it better men don't lie too well so woman can get away with it easier. The fact that they are also very good with time. Managing out to keep everyone in place and occupied. The special treat of their presence keeps him intrigued.

The player I dated he thought the was the man I mean tech he was all the woman wanted him and all the men wanted to be him. Such a smooth talker he loved RnB music which is a woman's love language I mean what better way to take a girl down than playing Silk. Meeting in my Bedroom was self-explanatory I mean that song can take anyone down panties are coming off. We met at a party, and he whispered to me "Out of all the woman in here you are the one who caught my eye" I laughed because I was never that easy to fall for bullshit. I turned to him and said, "Boy kill yaself." He was in shock "damn shorty I was saying how beautiful you are" he said. "Look I'm not interested I came out for a good time that's all" I said then I walked away. At the end of the night my girls and I walked out to my surprise he was waiting outside leaning on his car. "Lil mama lets go eat party is over and I know you're hungry." I looked at him and he seemed a little taller. Have you looked at someone and they seem a little taller anywho food is my love language so I said, "Sure we are hungry I don't know you so one of my girls must attend this breakfast if that's ok?" "Alright cool" he said so we left.

Fo the next couple of weeks he was calling all time picking me up taking me places I thought hey he seems to be worth the gold. He has been putting in work so let me give him a treat. I decided to give him some of these cookies and I wanted it to be special so made dinner and invited him over and showed nothing but love. It was definitely worth the wait and his stroke game was on point. He nutted quick I figured it was because he was waiting for so long boy how I was wrong.

After that night he didn't call as much, he was not as present things changed overnight. He would always say he was busy. The next thing I knew other woman was calling my phone talking about why her man is calling me. The nerve of these bitches but honestly the nerve of him. Getting me in beef I don't even want, have him sis. So that was pretty much the end for me. Two weeks later I seen him again and of course he was in another girl's face spitting his same rap I pulled her to the side and said "RUN."

BUMMIE

Aww where do I begin with this clown. This guy is the worst, I promise. The swag is real, and you will notice off hand he has nothing to offer. This man could ruin your life if you let him. Problem is no one will be able to compete with pillow talk and yes ladies this man will have it for you. See this bum ass dude has the best dick you ever had. The sex is going to be amazing however the bigger the dick the smaller the pockets. You are going to want to lick that lollipop daily, this is dangerous. Next thing you know you are doing things that are not you.

You are going to start cooking for this dude, cleaning the house, making sure new sheets are clean and candles are lit, the bedroom smells good. Like cherries because you are about to get popped. All he can do is bring the blunt and baby leg, and you are happy until you are not. All this good loving is terrible. Next thing you know he is walking around thinking he is a king. Now you guys are arguing all the time because you are the bread winner, he is living off you. Just a dick to calm you down boom you are pregnant. So, let's do the math, you slept with a bum now you have a bum baby daddy with a bum baby on the way make it make sense. Setting that baby up for failure. WAKE UP it is never that good.

Just a drunk hobo, a vagrant, a person who begs to get what he needs or wants. Which means, yeah, he is lit why cause his boys got the bottle. Will he have baby clothes for his newborn bum yup and it's called hand-me-downs. When I think about it, he may be the one to get abusive only because he cannot be anything, so he must tear you down to be lower than him. This is just my thoughts on how these types of men move. Have I dealt with a bum? Yup, and let's just say orgasm after orgasm and days of bliss. This dude was so fine body was ripped to stare at him was like looking at Jesse Williams and then I realized he ate my chocolate cookies. Yes, my damn cookies he ate all of them didn't save me not one, knowing this is my late-night snack. The bad part was he didn't have a car to go grab me anymore and the worse part was he didn't have the money to buy me any. Talk about a change of vision. My big eyes were wide open now we are in the house fighting about some damn cookies. He yelling talking, "You're tripping you're crazy," I said, "nah my dude you are broke and eating me out of house and home that third leg is not worth that much and no I don't want no damn head ya nasty dog." This did not last long, I promise you.

So, you do not get stuck in this situation; use it for what it is, then run Baby girl. Life is too short for this bum with three legs. Unless you want to give up your car while at work, pay for his habits and plan to stay on your back every night. The back part is not bad until it is. One last thing, if you think going on a date is going to happen it's not well unless you are paying for it. In the words of Forest Gump, "That's all I have to say about that."

Oh, don't think you Bummie woman are off the hook because there are so many of you. Honestly, this makes me so upset the woman who don't work and takes advantage of the system. Everything you have you were a whore for, nothing you have you didn't work for you just laid on your back for it. Men sleep with you because you are easy like Sunday morning Baby girl. You wake up every day to get cute just to meet some guy that may take care of your needs for the day. There is no motivation to do better, get better, nothing, you are content with doing nothing and having nothing.

The fact that you are waiting on "Prince Charming" is crazy don't get me wrong there are some men who will take care of these type of woman nine times out of ten he is ruling your whole life though. The fact that you have kids that are probably at your grandma's house or auntie's house makes you a bum pretty sure you are always out at the club though. Your homegirl is enabling you because she paid your way in, and you coned a sucka for some drinks. There is a 60% chance you woke up to that sucka the next morning. He woke up to a dirty house, a kid screaming, and a roach shit is crazy. Your everyday life is boring, so you live for the drama and gossip with nothing to lose fighting is always an option for you. If you are Ms. Bummie please get your life because you are running out of time getting into drama at 50 years old will not work for you doll you may break a bone the wrinkles kick in, kids are grown, and the food stamps will be cut. It's never too late to get a job however do you want to work at McDonald's at 50...? Yea think about it... moving on.

THE EATER

"Hmmmmmmm yummmmmmmy yes y'all know him ladies that head game is the winner. He is so damn good at it. Like what manual did he read to learn to slurp a woman up so well. This guy doesn't need to talk because anything out his mouth is just nasty, and I mean nasty. The crazy part is as woman one day we are going to fall for it. It's the curiosity it always kills the cat and let's just say by the end of the week he will be choking on hairballs. He takes pride in how well he can eat the passion and affection he shows with his mouth full is just talent. Pure talent.

Some may have good sex as well but from what I know they don't probably why they eat so well. Pretty sure he has had numerous women because this man does not see your face when he looks at you, he sees your legs wrapped around his face and inquires what your moan face will look like. He wants to see how nasty you will get with him. He will probably moan with you with as I mentioned before he enjoys pleasing you showing off his skills. This is the guy who is touchy feely when y'all meet. Just over doing it

I get it through the vagina is like fine wine. Fun fact your lady treasure's normal pH is less than 4.5 which is similar to the pH in wine. Just like wine men want to smell you taste you and be able to see it up close plus as I said before they want to hear your moaning. Yup we are addictive just like too much wine can get you drunk these men are literally getting drunk from eating our treasure box aka our fine wine. That high concentration of oestrogen tends to generate a male's sex drive. Studies show 77% of men love giving head its appealing to them however only 58% of woman want to enjoy the lollipop orally.

Don't get me wrong; there are plenty of woman who are eaters too. They absolutely love giving head. In my opinion it's about having that man at your mercy controlling them, pleasing with just a flick of the tongue. It's a turn on to watch your man grow from the work you are putting in. I mean how would you feel if he stayed soft the whole time? Women want to please their man. It brings pleasure to us to know you love all the work and effort. Talking nasty and being encouraging while your woman is pleasing you always helps just in case you didn't know that. I really think most woman get turned on from it. So keep that pole clean nobody asked for salt water or lent in their mouths. Some of you men are disgusting.

Men and woman get addicted to giving head because it pleasing the other person shows some type of emotions as well. Oh, and for you swallowers kudos to you. I am never babysitting your kids in my mouth or stomach. I get sick thinking about it. Y'all got some strong stomachs or maybe I should say strong throats. Either way you are holding get it yea holding. The problem is when you are an eater you become addicted, I think it's because it makes you feel good to make them feel good. You actually think you are doing something. Crazy part is when you become obsessed, she is now turned off.

Before I end this let's talk about the bootie eaters because playing with the pearl is one thing eating ass is a whole other story. Men have this thing about big butts I do not understand but hey I'm no guy, I get it though I wish my butt was big round and perky, but this doesn't stop a dude from trying to eat my ass these little cheeks will be over his face. I'm trying to suffocate his ass. Rimming can enhance intimacy and provide intense orgasms and can also open you up to more fantasies. Rimming feels different there is no half-assing it (pun intended). Honestly, I could not get too much into it because it may feel good initially nevertheless after a while it's just nasty. I mean you are eating my shit, slurping my bootie juice. I know it's not well; I mean does shit taste good? Then you want to kiss me with that mouth I don't think so. Kiss my ass literally. At this point it's normalized anyway.

From all I said once you get with this kind of guy it's hard to leave. He will never let you go sis. I know I was saying all the reasons why they enjoy it and reasons why they keep doing it even, so these dudes are crazy. To leave the freaky they crave is the hardest for them because guess what now they must find another female who enjoys the nastiness which seems easy but not really, it's a little harder. Think about it, now all he is doing is fantasizing about all the things y'all did in his brain like a movie. Now you have a Stalker......

STALK MUCH

In the words of Destiny Child:

"You make me wanna throw my pager out the window Tell MCI to cut the phone poles Break my lease so I can move 'Cause you're a bug a boo, a bug a boo I wanna put your number on the call block Have Gmail make my emails stop 'Cause you're a bug a boo You're buggin' what? you're buggin' who? You're buggin' me and don't you see it ain't cool Its not hot That you be callin' me stressin' me pagin' my beeper You're just non-stop and it's not hot That you be leaving' messages every ten minutes and then you stop by."

Sing that shit because these guys are just a headache. He ate his mind away, now he is a full-blown stalker. Yea you were having so much fun letting him eat as much pudding as he wanted sitting on his face every other night and now, he won't leave. See as I stated earlier it gets nasty and you don't want his nasty ass no more, but he can't get enough. Every night he is craving to eat your treasure box or that bootie. So as the song says he is calling all types of hours constantly popping up at your house or locations that you would see him before. Go ahead and change your number, he will find you on Facebook or Instagram. He will be all over your messenger and the worst is now he is trying talk to your friends not because he likes them, he just wants your attention.

In his mind this will make you jealous and eventually call him even if just to curse him out. He does not care if you are dating somebody, he is going to send those dick pictures anyway. Low key, he is a hater. All he wants is your ass back on his face. He thinks he loves you but really just lusting for you. There is no end game to this well not that I know of this can become a bit scary. They tend to get violent, for example he might see you out and about and grab you or try to fight the guy you are with, he is unpredictable.

Now the woman is even worse as we know woman can be dangerous fareal. There is no limit to what a woman may do. If you have a woman stalker beware and be ready. She may slash your tires, call your job, pop up to parties she may tell everyone you got a little dick just so other woman will talk to you. Oh, and she is checking your social media all day I pray another girl does not like any pictures or stats because she will be stalked as well. She may slash a few tires and bust your windows; you are not ready for the problems. Remember now you are dealing with the emotional creature you created.

Honestly, I am not sure which is worst the men or woman in this category. The men can be a lot to deal with however the woman can ruin your life. Per definition a stalker is someone who pursues someone obsessively and aggressively to the point of harassment. Well, we know harassment is the point because that is what it is. Some might find it cute until it's not. Also leading this crazy person on is never the best idea things can get dangerous.

I dealt with this guy who when we first met was a sweetheart such a gentleman. He would call to take me out and yes, I let him taste these goodies. He was so good at eating and sucking this pudding. I am not going to lie I let him come over about three times he enjoyed rimming so much I allowed him to do so not realizing how addicted he was getting. When I decided not to see talk to him anymore it was like he could not except that news. So, when I didn't answer the phone for him, he would pop up at my house. I cursed his ass out one thing I hate is for someone to pop up at my home. I remembered he popped up in the rain singing like we were in a relationship, and I gave a shit. I just cursed him out again. I moved thinking this would solve the problem. I also blocked his number so he would not have any contact with me. I thought wrong this place I live in is so small you can hide but not for long. I am not sure how he found my address, but he did, and he pulled up behind my car begging for another opportunity not to be with me but to eat this ass. This man was purely addicted to eating my ass guess I taste like strawberries. "Just give me a chance I just need one night" he would say. "Nah I'm good please leave," I said. He pulled off but as we know he still was never too far.

I got into a relationship thinking not thinking about this guy but one night around 3 am my phone rang. First, I was scared to answer even though I was doing anything to be nervous about but come on ladies and gentlemen if you were lying next to your lover and the phone rings at 3 am what are you going to do? My first thought was to end it but that would seem suspicious so since I didn't know the number, I answered oh why did I do that. Now he knows that it was still my number he hit the jackpot. For me my heart was pounding. I whispered, "what the fuck is wrong with you I am in a relationship and my man will not appreciate you calling especially this time of night." He response with the fake sexy deep voice. "Does he eat your ass like I do?" I just hung up the phone. Did this mutha f***ka call back in my brain I'm thinking is he serious he does not het the point. I almost let my dude answer maybe that would have stopped him but I do not like to cause drama, so I picked up and yelled, "stop calling my damn phone," and hung up and yes, this jerk called again so I put the phone on do not disturb but best believe that next morning my man was asking one thousand questions.

After that I changed my number, however, that was just an inconvenience must I go through all that just to get away from someone. Respect what I ask please just leave me alone why is this so hard. Changing and moving is crazy but guess what that is what happens when you let someone get attached that you really don't like. Letting them taste the goodies just let them be and move to the next.

FLASHY ZADDY

Bitch I'm blind it's so hard to see through this guy he is too damn bright. He has 10 chains on a bunch of rings and is ready to spend whatever he can on the punanee. Most people call this guy a sugar daddy is a man who lavishes on young woman with gifts for favors whatever favors they negotiate. This doesn't mean he has low self-esteem; it just means he doesn't want anything but someone to do whatever he asks. Money is the motivation for both parties to participate in these encounters. Don't look down on her for getting that money half you bitche's fucking for free so don't be mad or jealous cause she getting paid for the same thing you do for nothing.

Although he is paying for your time this may be the issue. One thing about Mr. flashy Daddy he wants attention, why do you think he is so flashy. The problem is he is not getting the attention he craves. This guy is probably married with kids, so home life is not appealing anymore. So, when he wants your time everything else is out the window. You are fulfilling what he is craving and not getting at home. Although at first, it's all fun and money until you start really feeling like a whore. Which eventually will start messing with your mental unless you don't care however most woman will eventually care. Now you must make the decision do you want to keep selling your body or move on. This is not as easy as it seems that money comes in handy, and the dick might be good. I cannot give you answers to that sorry those are your morals and conscience you must deal with.

Woman can be flashy mommas it's just different. Flashy mommas want affection and to be touched. They need their self-esteem back for whatever reason they are not getting any. These women are not even asking for sex they just want you to tell them they are beautiful and sexy. They want a slap on the bootie while they make you dinner and all of this will be in private no public anything. The payments from them are more than money due to our nature they may upgrade your wardrobe shit she might upgrade his whole life. Men will love this I mean what man wouldn't a woman who wants nothing but to spoil them with no commitment talk about a guy's dream.

I used to have a flashy daddy he was too flashy though it was a bit weird for me. I like my man looking good but a man who cares what others think is crazy to me shows insecurity. He would pay for my time anytime he wanted to see me. Sometimes I would charge for the phone conversation shit time is time. The plus was I got to get dressed and go to so many beautiful places. A girl loves to get cute and go out. Plus, he was a gentleman, he opened doors and pulled out chairs. He made sure I was noticed by all those who noticed him. He had to show off his diamond. I realized this guy had everything so why was he paying for my attention and then he dropped them drawls. Poor baby had all big things because he was missing the most important big thing.

As nice as he was guessing he felt no woman would ever really love him. Let's be honest what man wants to marry a gold digger as soon as you become broke, she will be gone. This is the negative for the man and a woman. No one man or woman wants to be used however in this situation isn't that the point? If you get into this situation my advice is make the rules very clear, you can't involve emotion, and both parties must know the role they are playing. That way there is no confusion, and no one gets hurt. But this is your choice listen to me or not hey I'm no expert by law but by experience trust me let's just say I'M AN OG.

NARCISSIST

If you are this person you are going to be upset, do I care? Not really if the shoe fits well, you know the rest of that statement. This best way to describe this person man or woman is selfish. I do not mean the regular selfish like they don't want to share food I mean selfish all about them selfish. This person has a lack of empathy, manipulative, entitled, gas lighting little bitches. Playing the victim comes natural to them and shifting the blame is almost too easy. When they apologize it's never sincere and you will hear nothing but things to justify why they did whatever they did. Excuses with an apology is not an apology at all. It's like saying "I am sorry for punching you in the face, but your face is too big and was in my way when I swung." The fantasy world they live in is delusional and no one lives there.

The consistent praise they desire is ridiculous; their sense of self-importance is too much for most to bare. You want to know the crazy part this is considered a disorder yup technically this is a personality disorder. I swear they will give a pill for anything. The definition is: having an excessive or erotic interest in oneself and physical appearance, which basically means it's all about themselves. They are unable to recognize the needs and feelings of others. They are arrogant and brag a lot very conceited when secretly they are ashamed, insecure, and have a fear of being exposed as a failure. They will not take on challenges and are not good with change. They tend to get depressed and moody if they are not perfect. Such a hard life to live trying to be perfect all the time I would be going crazy too.

The guy I dated yelled all the time. He couldn't have a conversation without sounding as if everything I said was wrong. Always trying to prove a point for no reason. At first it was fun due to the fact I love a little debate unfortunately it would become an argument. How can you have a debate with someone who cannot respect your opinion or at least agree to disagree. Everything I said or did was wrong, telling him this is me wasn't enough because if we are not perfect it was not right in his eyes. I am far from perfect so being yelled at all the time the little things were becoming a bit abusive. Verbally not physically however abuse is abuse if you read my first book "Love of Abuse" (if not cop that) you would understand.

As I stated earlier the woman are the same as the men in this category however 7.7% of men will suffer from NPD while only 4.8% of woman may have NPD. NPD is the Narcissistic Personality Disorder I told y'all this is a real thing. Now for the woman you will see the same traits there are a few differences for example these NPD women are very petty and can never admit when they are wrong. They are self-centered and are addicted to social status and are extremely shallow. They are materialistic and vain they can become obsessed with getting likes and followers online. These are dangerous, they do not take criticism too well and are subject to getting cosmetic procedures dieting may even pick up some unhealthy dangerous habits.

Even the way they dress the woman will dress seductively put on a lot of makeup. These women are sensitive due to deep down they are insecure with a low self-esteem, which, as I stated before, is dangerous. That movie Mean Girls well when you think of Regina George think narcissistic women. She actually is a perfect example; she was vain, mean, always belittling people. I'm not sure who is worse, the men or the women; in my opinion, they are both too much to handle. It's just stressful and not worth the time to deal with all the drama.

Be at peace and if you see these traits do not give them the time unless you like to argue and have drama all the time. I don't want to say run I am going to say just go blind and deaf however these people are everywhere work family school or in a relationship. It's like being a groupie for the rest of your life. Whatever works for you hey it's our life not mine.

Them/They

Alright please do not hate me for this chapter, however I cannot leave them out. Now according to the Oxford Dictionary, the pronouns "them /they" has been used since year1375 and I do mean for a person not in a plural form. Honestly, I would have never known that if I didn't do my research kind of blew my mind. This is a gender-neutral pronoun some of us use these terms to identify themselves. Which is confusing to me I really do not get it but to each its own my only thing with this is why are y'all doing things that make no sense.

Let's talk about it. You said this is you right you are dressed as a stud covering all your woman parts wearing strap ons but then get pregnant. So, you are looking like a boy pregnant fyi sis men don't want to be pregnant only gay men do which for obvious reasons they want to be a female. So, are you really being real to yourself? You want to be a boy but you still getting fucked like the rest of these hoes. Somebody help me understand. Then woman may date a stud thinking they are going to be better but nope they want to be a dude they not shit either. I get it I always if I could be a guy for one day I would get my dick sucked I want to know what the big deal is. Women love head but to men it's like winning a million dollars. Having a fake one sucked won't help me.

I understand you don't want to be labeled or called a certain sex or gender but if you are going to be something play your part why make it so confusing. The gay men whom I love the only thing that kills me with y'all is y'all are too extra. Like snapping your fingers and neck way too much not all women are ghetto fabulous. Not all women stir up tea yes, we love the tea, but we don't always start drama. Being a woman is not about being loud and obnoxious Shanaynay was a fictional character. Then you want to date a girl you became a woman to date a woman why not be a man?

Look be whoever you want I love all people no matter what the decision you make or what you wear or who you decide to be anyone who knows me knows I love all people. I just need some clarification on what are the rules and while we are on the subject who is the person who makes these terms? Every month it's a new one. At first it was LGBTQ now there are so many more terms it's hard to keep up I am just saying. And whatever you decide to be stick with it because it's a lot to see a stud pregnant. I got one more question if a man fucks a stud does that make him gay? Honestly I think it's a valid question. Don't get me wrong there are some fine ass studs, but I feel like they are pretty and handsome at the same time however that is to me a female to a man it's like looking at a cute boy, right? Hey these are just my thoughts I am no psychologist these are just my thoughts and wonders.

Anyway, to them/ they keep doing you boo boo as I said before curiosity always kills the cat in your cases I do mean literally. You got curious and now you are not who we thought you were originally but maybe someone better. Whatever makes you happy I'm here for it. I just wish it was easier for us to understand the meaning please don't make any more terminology I have taken so many classes, and I still don't have them all and believe me I have tried out of my respect and love for the community I have tried. I hope you are smiling and laughing because I mean no offense I am just one of many curious bystanders. Alright enough on that.

SMALL FRY

Heeeeeeeeeeeeeeeeeeeeeeeyyyyyy my little friends. I know y'all out there my little peanuts. You know who I am talking to or about. Don't be shy, speak up and hold your head up high. This term, 'small fry,' in slang means for those who do not know is someone or something considered insignificant or minor aka unimportant. But let this be clear I am talking about the guys with the small fry aka baby penis, aka needle dicks, aka bay carrots, aka weenies all size matters. Do not think you are not important matter fact repeat after me, "you are kind, you are smart, you are important" Yes you are baby.

These small fries always have a big truck driving with little stubby fingers. They will always go extra because they feel they need to. These types of guys have long four play will always buy the big bottles smoke you under the weather and will eat the box until its dry. You got it give them their props they definitely know how to clear a plate if you get my drift. Don't get me wrong some can screw very well and if you are emotionally attached to that person, you may feel it. You may feel that needle prick.

I had a small fry he was cool and funny. We had a great vibe and yes, he had a nice truck. He was protective over me, and the boy could fight probably because he had a lot of anger built up inside. I assume. I would have never thought he was so little by the way he was but baby when the four play was over, and he climbed on top of me something was not right. I waited for that first initial pump. I should have known something was wrong when he kept fingering me, annoying like get to it already. By the time he was ready he came so quick it's like ok little pinky at least take your time geesh.

The second time we had sex (yes, I tried again I said he was cool) he started again with the great head sucked my pretty apples and proceeded to jump on top of me. Except this time was different not sure why, but that shit was so good. I felt every pump every stroke I think he even made it to a wall. I can't explain what happened because I honestly don't know, maybe because I liked his personality, maybe the head was better or maybe it was a "hennything" kind of night. Either way the pencil was breaking the paper baby. I was so proud, and things really were working out we broke up for other reasons. What I will say again is don't be shy guys about that little wee wee somebody going to love it.

On another note, I think us as woman should not fake the funk with these men. If you cannot feel him, tell him. Why fake it so he can go screw the next girl and she comes up short. I think the men need to know if they are not pleasing. When you get a new job, you must train, right well same thing for the fellas' ladies if you get a guy who has everything you like don't fake moaning and lying using the rose after he put in what he thinks is work. Tell him he sucks, and you need more train him to be the lover you want him to be. If he quits and get sensitive hey that's on him, he can take that baby dick to the next. Now if he stays and learns his craft marry that man.

THOUGHTS

I hope you enjoyed this and learned something from it. As I stated before, I am no doctor; I am not a psychologist; I have no degrees in relationships, but I have a lot of experience. There is no shame here in my Mariah Lynn voice:

"Once upon a time, not long ago, I was a hoe. I have no shame there because technically I was a pimp and emotionless. I treated men like dirt and did what I wanted, and these are some of the men I ran across. I know a few will relate, and some of y'all may not. However, to keep it 100 every woman has a 'hoe stage,' and those who didn't well pretty sure you are in a relationship that you don't even want because you don't know what you want. The statement you can't turn a hoe into a housewife is a lie. These dudes are making wives of these hoes every day. Body count means nothing, don't let anyone tell you different. It's on you. Men fuck more than one woman all the time and nobody cares its different cause who has an innie vs. an outie man please kill that noise. Be happy, do you learn from these fools and try to make the best of any situation.

Finally, NEVER SETTLE; life is too short to not be loved and fucked good......................"

Also by Shatima Jones

Love of Abuse

A raw and deeply moving memoir that explores the resilience of the human spirit in the face of emotional, physical, and mental abuse. Shatima Jones shares her powerful story with unflinching honesty, offering readers a path to healing and hope. *Perfect for readers who are on their own journey to self-discovery and empowerment.*

Available at major online bookstores worldwide.